D1240803

BUNRAKU

written by Tokio Oga
photographs by Koichi Mimura
translated and edited
       by Don Kenny

CONTENTS

(Cover Photo)   Lady Shizuka in YOSHITSUNE AND
THE THOUSAND CHERRY TREES
(Yoshitsune Senbon-Zakura)

■ materials and information provided by
the Bunraku Association

1 — Osome in THE NEW BALLAD SINGER ▶
(Shinpan Utazaemon)

B U N R A K U

by Tokio Oga

photographs by Koichi Mimura

translated by Don Kenny

© All rights reserved. No. 44 of Hoikusha's Color Books
Series. Published by Hoikusha Publishing Co., Ltd., 17-13,
1-chome, Uemachi, Higashi-ku, Osaka, 540 Japan. ISBN
4-586-54044-3. First Edition in 1984. Printed in JAPAN

THE FAITHFUL FORTY-SEVEN

(Kana-dehon Chushingura)
premiered in 1748   11 Acts
by Takeda Izumo   Photos 2–19

3 – Prologue (Act 1)
Helmet Inspection Scene
Kaoyo inspects the Helmet

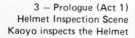

2

2 — Prologue
(Act 1)
Helmet Inspection
Scene   Moronao
leers lasciviously
at Kaoyo

3

3

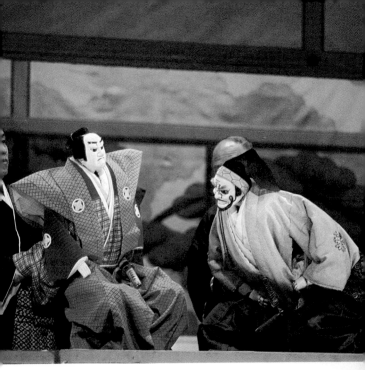

5 — Act 3   Wounding Scene   Moronao taunts Hangan

◀ 4 — Act 3   Back Gate Scene
Okaru delivers a Letter
to Her Lover Kanpei

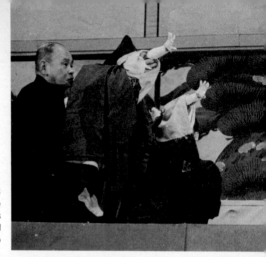

6 — Act 3
Wounding Scene
Hangan draws
His Sword
on Moronao

7 — Act 4
Hangan's Suicide
Yuranosuke
makes up His
Mind to revenge
Hangan's Death

8 — Act 4   Hangan's Suicide   Hangan prepares
to make the Final Thrust

9 — Act 4   Back Gate Scene ▶
Yuranosuke leaves Hangan's Mansion
determined to take Revenge

10 — Act 5
Yamazaki Highway
Okaru's Aged Father
Yoichibei meets
the Trecherous
Sadakuro on the
Road

11 — Act 5
Yamazaki Highway
Kanpei takes
a Wallet filled
with 50 Ryo
from Sadakuro's
Dead Body

▲

12 — Act 6
Yoichibei's Home
Okaru and Her
Mother anxiously
await Yoichibei's
Return

13 — Act 7   The Ichiriki Tea House   Okaru reads

Yuranosuke's Letter through Her Mirror across a Courtyard

**14 — Act 7   The Ichiriki Tea House   Heiemon tells
Okaru of Kanpei's Suicide**

16 — Act 8   Travel Scene   Tonase lightly teases Konami
as they travel

17 — Act 9   The Yamashina Residence   Konami is surprised to see Her Father Honzo here

18 — Act 9   The Yamashina Residence   Konami and Tonase
determine to commit Suicide as Konami has been rejected

19 — Act 9   The Yamashina Residence   Honzo runs himself
through on Rikiya's Spear for the sake of His Daughter
Konami

20 — Act 3   Mountain Scene on the Yoshino
River   Hinadori tries to get a glimpse of Her
Lover Kuganosuke across the Yoshino River

PROPER UPBRINGING OF A YOUNG LADY AT MOUNT IMOSE
(Imose-Yama Onna Teikin)
premiered in 1771   5 Acts   by Chikamatsu Hanji
Photos 20 — 26

21 — Act 3 Mountain Scene on Yoshino River
        The Tragic Double Suicide of Hinadori and Kuga-
        nosuke brings Their Feuding Fathers to a Recon-
        ciliation

22 — Act 4   The Sugi Wine Shop   Laborers
drink heartily after digging a New Well

天照大神

23 — Act 4   The Sugi Wine Shop   Omiwa
and Her Lover Motome decide not to
part no matter what may happen

24 — Act 4   The Sugi Wine Shop   Omiwa
hurries Home after School

25 — Act 4   Travel Scene   Omiwa and Motome set out
to run away together

26 — Act 4   The Golden Mansion Scene   Fisherman Fukashichi
relates His Story

YOSHITSUNE AND THE THOUSAND CHERRY TREES

(Yoshitsune Senbon-zakura)

premiered in 1747   5 Acts   by Takeda Izumo

Photos 27 – 33

28 — Act 2   Daimotsu Bay Scene   General Tomomori ties
himself to a Huge Anchor to commit Suicide by
drowning in lament of His Defeat in Battle

◀ 27 — Act 2   Daimotsu Bay Scene   Lady Suke laments
the Sad Fate of the Infant Emperor Antoku

27

29 — Act 3   The Sushi Shop   Osato tells Koremori and

His Wife of Her Sad Tale of Love for One far above her in Social Rank

31 — Act 4   Mount Yoshino Travel Scene
The Fox Genkuro listens sadly to the
Sound of the Drum covered with the Skin
of His Parents as it is played by Lady
Shizuka

33 — Act 4   The Kawazura Mansion Scene   The Fox who had
disguised himself as Tadanori reveals His True Form and
tells His Story

 ◄ 32 — Act 4   Mount Yoshino Travel Scene   The Warrior Tada-
nori protects Lady Shizuka on Her Journey

A PICTURE BOOK OF THE TAIKO TALES
(Ehon Taiko Ki)
premiered in 1799   13 Acts
by Chikamatsu Yanagi
Photos 34 – 40

35 — Act 10   Amagasaki   Tojiro makes up His Mind to ▶
go to Battle and fight to the Death

34 — Act 6   The Myoshin Temple   Mitsuhide
relates His True Purpose as he writes His Death
Poem

34

36 – Act 10   Amagasaki
Hatsugiku says a Reluctant
Farewell to Tojiro as she
dresses him for Battle

38 — Act 10   Amagasaki   Mitsuhide praises the
Bravery and Fidelity of the Two Young
People

37 — Act 10 Amagasaki
Hatsugiku watches
sadly as Tojiro sets
out for the Battle-
field

▼ 39 — Act 10 Amagasaki
Hatsugiku weeps
when Tojiro comes
back from the Battle
seriously wounded

40 — Act 10   Amagasaki   Mitsuhide climbs up into a Pine Tree
to see how close the Enemy has approached

41 —Act 4   Foxfire Scene
Princess Yaegaki runs out after Her
Beloved Katsuyori with the Family
Heirloom Helmet in Her Hand

TWENTY-FOUR EXPRESSIONS OF FILIAL LOVE
(Honcho Niju-shi Ko)
premiered in 1766   5 Acts
by Chikamatsu Hanji   Photos 41 — 44

43 — Act 4
Ten Incense Scene
Katsuyori and
Nureginu listen as
Princess Yaegaki claims
she is not in Love with
Her Lord

42 — Act 3   Bamboo Shoot Digging Scene   Two
Brothers fight over a Mysterious Box they have
found in the Ground

44 — Act 4   Foxfire Scene   Princess Yaegaki rushes to Her
Lover's Side aided by the Fox who is a Divine Messenger

45 — Act 2   The Seal Breaking Scene   Umegawa realizes
the Depth of Chubei's Love when she learns of the
Situation he has gotten himself into for her

A MESSENGER FROM HADES
(Meido no Hikyaku)
premiered in 1711   3 Acts
by Chikamatsu Monzaemon   Photos 45 — 48

Chubei becomes overexcited as he listens to
Hachiemon speak

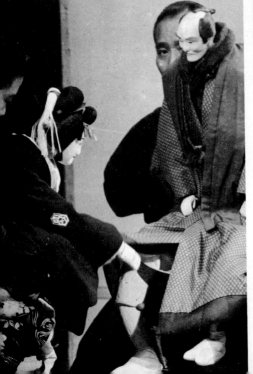

◀ 48 — Act 3   Niikuchi Village
     Scene   Chubei's Father
   Magoemon is moved as he
   hears Umegawa's Story

DOUBLE SUICIDE AT SONEZAKI
(Sonezaki Shinju)
premiered in 1703   3 Acts
by Chikamatsu Monzaemon
Photos 49 — 52

49 — Act 1   At Ikutama Shrine   Ohatsu and Tokubei have a
Happy Reunion

50 — Act 2   The Tenmaya Tea House   Ohatsu signals to
Tokubei with Her Foot Her Decision to die with him

49

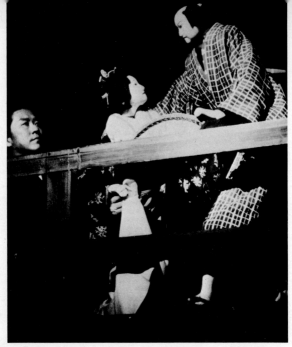

51 — Act 3   The Trip to Tenjin Woods   Ohatsu
and Tokubei travel toward Their Death

52 — Act 3   Tenjin Woods   Ohatsu and Tokubei
          commit Double Suicide

THE NEW BALLAD SINGER

(Shinpan Uta-zai-mon)
premiered in 1780
2 Acts
by Chikamatsu Hanji
Photo 53

53 — Act 1　The Zama
Shrine Scene　Osome
and Hisamatsu declare
Their Hopeless Love
for each other

52

▼ 55 — Act 1   Kawasho Magoemon,
         Koharu's older Brother, disguised as a
         Samurai, tries to discover Her True
         Intent

DOUBLE SUICIDE AT TEN-NO-AMIJIMA *(Shinju Ten-no-Amijima)* premiered in 1720 3 Acts by Chikamatsu Monzaemon Photos 54 — 57

▲ 54 — Act 2   The Tenma Paper Shop   Osan's Father Gozaemon scolds Jihei severely and takes Osan Home with Him

56 — Act 2   The Tenma Paper Shop   Osan pleads tearfully with Her Husband Jihei

57 — Act 3   The Yamato Tea House Scene   Koharu and Jihei
sadly make up Their Minds to die together

58 — Act 3   The Lion Castle   Watonai is
determined to save the Family Honor

THE BATTLE OF KOKUSENYA
(Kokusenya Kassen)
premiered in 1715   5 Acts
by Chikamatsu Monzaemon
Photo 58

TAIHEIKI TALES TOLD WITH WHITE GO STONES
(Go Taiheiki Shiraishi-Banashi)
premiered in 1780   11 Acts
by Utei Enba   Photo 60

59 — Act 6   The Yoshiwara Ageya Tea House
The Courtesan Miyagino and Her Sister
Shinobu meet for the first time in a long time

60 — Act 8   The Draw Window   Nuregami's
Mother shaves His Head to expiate His
Crime assisted by His Brother's Wife
Ohaya

THE DIARY OF TWO BUTTERFLIES IN THE GAY QUARTERS

(Futatsu Chocho Kuruwa Nikki)
premiered in 1749   9 Acts
by Takeda Izumo   Photo 59

61 — Act 4   The Private Elementary School Scene
Matsuo and His Wife have substituted the Life
of Their Child for that of Their Lord's Child
and set out to commit Suicide after Their
Mission has been accomplished

MORALISTIC TALES OF SUGAWARA MICHIZANE
(Sugawara Denju Tenarai Kagami)
premiered in 1746   5 Acts
by Takeda Izumo   Photos 61 — 62

62 — Act 4   The Private Elementary
School Scene   The Decision to
commit Double Suicide with His Wife
is full of Complications for the Ailing
Matsuo

THE CHRONICLE OF THE BATTLE HELMET AT DANNOURA

(Dan-no-ura Kabuto Gunki)

premiered in 1732   5 Acts

by Bunkodo   Photo 63

**OLD
BROCADE
PICTURES OF
MOUNT
KAGAMI**
*(Kagami Yama
Kokyo no
Nishiki-E)*
premiered in 1782
11 Acts
by Yo Yotai
Photo 64

64 — Act 6   Flower Viewing Scene
The Evil Lady Iwafuji torments
the Maid Onoe

◀ 63 — Act 3   The Koto Torture Scene   The Courtesan
Akoya searches for Her Lover Kagekiyo

THE
SUBSCRIPTION
LIST
(Kanjincho)
premiered
in 1840
1 Act
by Namiki
Gohei III
Photos 65 — 66

66 — Benkei dances for joy after passing through the Barrier Gate

◀ 65 — Togashi threatens Benkei

EARLY WAR TALES OF ICHINOTANI
(Ichinotani Futaba Gunki)
premiered in 1731   5 Acts
by Namiki Sosuke   Photo 67

67 — Act 3   The Kumagai Battlefront Mansion   Kumagai
holds a Severed Head up for Yoshitsune's Inspection

68 — Act 7   Behind the Tenement House
Danshiki battles bravely

THE TALE OF THE SUMMER FESTIVAL IN OSAKA
(Natsu Matsuri Naniwa Kagami)
premiered in 1745   9 Acts
by Namiki Senryu   Photo 68

69 — Act 1   Matahei, the Stutterer   Matahei dances
for joy upon being entrusted with an Important
Mission

INCENSE REQUIEM FOR A COURTESAN
(Keisei Hangon Ko)
premiered in 1708   3 Acts
by Chikamatsu Monzaemon
Photo 69

70 — Act 6   Numazu   Jubei looks on sadly as His Father ▶
Heisaku dies

A TRIP THROUGH THE IGA MOUNTAINS

(Iga-Goe Dochu Sugoroku)

premiered in 1783   10 Acts

by Chikamatsu Hanji   Photos 70 – 72

72 — Act 6   Numazu   Jubei
and Oyone meet with
Kyusaku

THE ETERNAL WEIR IN THE KATSURA RIVER
(Katsura-Gawa Renri no Shigarami)
premiered in 1776
2 Acts
by Suga Sensuke
Photo 73

73 — Act 2   The Sash
Shop   Ohan peeks
sadly out the door as
she thinks of Her Sad
Fate of being married
to a Man twice Her
Age

73

74 — Act 3   The Oil Shop
Scene   Manno throws
Mitsugu out of the Shop
and insults him

AN ISE SONG OF THE SLEEPING SWORD OF LOVE
(Ise Ondo Koi no Netaba)
premiered in 1769   4 Acts
by Chikamatsu Tokuzo   Photos 74 — 76

75 — Act 3　The Oil Shop Scene
Manno laughs derisively at
Fukuoka Mitsugu in front
of Okon

▼ 76 — Act 3　The Oil Shop
Scene　Mitsugu attacks
Manno

77 — Act 10
Shigenoi Parts
with Her Child
She takes a Final
Glimpse of Her
Child through
Her Mirror

A COLORFUL BRIDLE FOR A BELOVED BRIDE
(Koi Nyobo Somewake Tazuna)
premiered in 1751   13 Acts
by Yoshida Kanshi   Photo 77

78 — The Unagidani Scene   Hachirobei sets out for Home after ▶
an Aborted Attempt to discover the True Feelings of a
Woman who has rejected him

THE SHARK SCABBARD OF SPITE UNDER THE CHERRY BLOSSOMS
(Sakura Tsuba Urami no Samezaya)
premiered in 1774   number of acts and author unknown
Photos 78 – 79

**THE OUCHI TALE OF
ASHIYA DOMAN**
*(Ashiya Doman Ouchi
Kagami)*
premiered in 1734   5 Acts
by Takeda Izumo
Photos 80 – 81

79 — The Unagidani Scene
Ohan sadly explains Her
Mother's Intent after
Hachirobei has killed her

▼ 80 — Act 4   Kuzunoha's
Parting with Her Child
Doshi and Shoji look on as
Kuzunoha inscribes Her
Parting Poem on the Paper
Doors

81 — Act 4   Kuzunoha's Parting with Her Child
Kuzunoha reveals Her True Fox Nature
before she leaves

82 — Act 2   The Wine Shop   Osono reads Her Husband's
Will sadly

THE WOMAN IN A GAUDY DANCE COSTUME
(Hade Sugata Onna Maiginu)
premiered in 1772   3 Acts
by Takemoto Saburobei   Photos 82 — 84

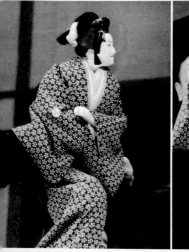

83 — Act 2   The Wine Shop
Hanbei accepts Arrest in place
of His Son as His Wife Osono
and Sogan look on in a State
of Shock

▼ 84 — Act 2   The Wine Shop
This sequence shows Osono's
Famous Lament over Her
Husband's Arrest

85 — Act 4   The
        Kanzaki Ageya
        Tea House
        The Courtesan
        Umegae, who
        has sold her-
        self to the Tea
        House out of
        Love, washes
        Her Hands in
        Her Most
        Famous Scene

ALPHABETICAL TALES OF PROSPERITY AND DECLINE
(Hirakana Seisui Ki)
premiered in 1739   5 Acts
by Bunkodo   Photo 85

THREE GENERATIONS AT KAMAKURA
(Kamakura Sandai Ki)
premiered in 1718   5 Acts
by Chikamatsu Hanji (?)
Photos 86 — 87

86 — Act 3   Kinugawa Village Scene   Princess Toki's Love
deepens as she cares for the Wounded Miuranosuke

THE FRONTLINE BATTLE MANSION OF OMI GENJI
(Omi Genji Senjin Yakata)
premiered in 1769   9 Acts
by Miyoshi Shoraku   Photo 88

89 — Act 2   Gappo's
Retreat   Lady
Tamate returns
home drawn by
Her Deep Love

GAPPO OF SESSHU AND HIS DAUGHTER TSUJI
(Sesshu Gappo-ga-Tsuji)
premiered in 1773   2 Acts
by Suga Sensuke   Photo 89

90 — Act 2   The Sukiya Tea Room   Gonza comes
for a Secret Message late at night and meets with
an Unexpected Incident

GONZA OF THE SPEAR IN A MANY-LAYERED COSTUME
(Yari no Gonza Kasane Katabira)
premiered in 1717   3 Acts
by Chikamatsu Monzaemon   Photo 90

A TALE OF THE GAY QUARTERS
(Kuruwa Bunsho)
premiered in 1780   1 Act
author unknown   Photo 92

92 — At the Yoshidaya Tea House
Yugiri and Izaemon have a Lover's Spat
in spite of it being Their First Meeting in
a long time

A RECENT STORY OF RIVALRY IN KAWARA
(Chikagoro Kawara no Tatehiki)
premiered in 1782   3 Acts
by Tamekawa Sosuke   Photo 91

91 — Act 2   Horikawa   The Blind
Mother comes out with the Monkey
Trainer Yojiro to cheer Oshun and
Denbei as they set out on Their
Journey toward Double Suicide

THE COURTESAN AT THE STRAITS OF AWA
(Keisei Awa no Naruto)
premiered in 1695   10 Acts
by Chikamatsu Hanji   Photo 93

93 — Act 8   At Jurobei's Home   Oyumi laments not being able to announce to Otsuru that she is Her Mother

94 — Act 2   The Kochiya Tea House
Yohei's Mother scolds him for His
Delinquent Behavior

MURDER OF A WOMAN IN A HELL OF OIL
(Onna Goroshi Abura no Jigoku)
premiered in 1721   3 Acts
by Chikamatsu Monzaemon   Photo 94

THE MIRACLE AT TSUBOSAKA
(Tsubosaka Kannon Reigen Ki)
premiered in 1879   1 Act
by Sengajo   Photo 95

95 — At Sawaichi's Home   Osato
declares Her Love for Her Husband
Sawaichi

96 — Act 3   Hyuga Island   Kagekiyo refuses to admit that
Itotaki is His Daughter out of pride and concern for Her
Wellbeing

THE YASHIMA DIARY OF KAGEKIYO'S DAUGHTER
(Musume Kagekiyo Yashima Nikki)
premiered in 1764   5 Acts
by Wakatake Tekkyu   Photo 96

95

97 — Young Man *(Waka-otoko)* 　　98 — Courtesan *(Keisei)*

99 — Old Father-in-law *(Ojuto)* 　100 — Bad Young Man *(Oni-waka)*

PRACTICAL ELEMENTS

Bunraku is a traditional performing art that consists of a NARRATOR reading a Gidayu Joruri libretto to the accompaniment of a SHAMISEN while PUPPETS handled by three PUPPETEERS each act out the story on the stage. When these three types of performers achieve a harmonious rhythm the resulting effect is dazzling indeed. One of the best examples of such a performance is the now legendary incident in which the mutual concentration between the Narrator, the Shamisen Player, and the Chief Handler was so high that at the climax of the scene they were performing the puppeteer's sash ripped in two. Even though this incident took place at the end of the 19th century, Bunraku fans still tell the story as though they had seen it themselves, as a matter of great amazement at the wonderful artistry of the art of Bunraku.

This chapter is a brief analysis of the practical elements of Bunraku including the three types of performers, the puppets, and the stage.

The Narrator

In Kabuki those born into traditional actor families are given first priority in casting, leaving very little chance for outsiders to obtain major roles, but in Bunraku, everything depends entirely upon the actual ability of the individual. The fame of one's father or the support of one's teacher are of no account, for this is a world where one's ability is the only thing that brings success. For this reason, training is of a level of severity that cannot be imagined unless actually experienced.

The breadth of training necessary is particularly

evident in the case of the Narrator, for he must not only describe the scene where the action is taking place and the storyline, but he must also be able to perform any and all types of characters and all human emotions all by himself and sometimes simultaneously. In Kabuki, all an actor has to do is memorize the dialogue of a single character, and if he happens to forget a line on the stage, a prompter will help him out. Of course, the Bunraku Narrator does have his text in front of him at all times, so he does not have to memorize his lines perfectly either, but the responsibility for all verbal effects lies on his shoulders alone all the time he is on stage.

Vocal requirements for Gidayu Joruri Narrators include first the ability to speak with an Osaka accent, plus three different types of vocalizations — dialogue (*kotoba*), narration in rhythm with the Shamisen accompaniment (*jiai*), and melodic chanting (*fushi*). The dialogue is spoken without accompaniment, the rhythmical narration is used for explaining scenery and setting moods with half-sung half-spoken words delivered at various pitches and in rhythm with the Shamisen accompaniment, and the melodic chanting is sung in a clear voice for such highly emotional scenes as that of a young couple making their way toward the place where they will commit double suicide. The lustrous, full, and clear tones of the Narrator's voice in this melodic chanting style never fail to enchant an audience.

The Narrator sits on his knees with his feet flexed so that his body is supported by his toes and a very small, very low stool call a 'Shichibei.' He wraps a very wide sash around his hips and lower abdomen, and inserts a small bag full of sand or beans into the front of that sash. This bag is known as an 'otoshi' and its purpose is to provide greater support for the voice which is produced through very strong abdominal breath control. If the voice were produced with only the throat and the lips, it would not project sufficiently for the words to be heard by the audience, and the voice would become hoarse in less than three days of training. At the same time, the shaping of the mouth for pronunciation is extremely important in the creating of different moods and characters. But Narrators are taught that they must approach each role from the inside rather than attempt a surface imitation of such roles as young girls. It is said that if this approach is taken, the resulting voice will naturally come to sound like the role being played at any given time.

There are two basic narration styles which are known as the 'Eastern Style' and the 'Western Style,' the origin of which is discussed in the following chapter on history. But a number of variations have been developed over the years by famous Narrators for specific scenes or characters, and these were adopted and passed down to the present. They have been kept because of their excellence as ready-made shortcuts for the building of a vivid presentation, and they all bear the names of their originators.

Some examples that come immediately to mind are the monologue of Omitsu in the Nozaki Village scene of 'The New Ballad Singer' (*Shinpan Uta-zai-mon*) in the style of Kumi-dayu; the dark narration to the bright shamisen accompaniment for the 'Wine Shop' scene of 'The Woman in a Gaudy Dance Costume' (*Hade Sugata Onna Maiginu*) in the style of Bunya-dayu; and the Mountain Scene on the Yoshino River in 'Proper Upbringing of a Young Lady at Mount Imose' (*Imose Yama Onna Teikin*) with the father of the young man on the stage right side of the river narrated in the subdued style of Some-dayu and the father of the girl on the stage left side of the river done in the gorgeously elegant style of Haru-dayu — a contrast which greatly aids the dramatic buildup and climax of the scene.

With such a broad spectrum of variations on the basic narrative style, the training requirements imposed upon the Narrators are great indeed. But one of the strong motivations for mastering all the basic style techniques as well as those of the variations is the fact that the possibility of creating one's own fresh interpretation of a scene or a character remains open at all times. An example of this phenomenon in modern times is Yama-shiro-dayu's interpretation of 'Gappo of Sesshu and His Daughter Tsuji' (*Sesshu Gappo-ga-Tsuji*).

Some complaints have been heard that it takes far too much time for the theatergoer to learn to appreciate such high levels of training, but the fact is that the training is only a tool to be used in making the dramatic content easily understood and moving to even the casual theater-goer. Thus the art of Bunraku, as all other true arts, is structured in such a way that it can be appreciated on a large range of levels if its performers are of truly high quality, for aside from a number of obsolete words in the lyrics and some outmoded customs and ethics, the stories tell of the basic nature of the human heart that goes beyond all bounds of time and space to appeal with equal strength to people of all ages including the present one. It is the responsibility of all Bunraku performers to hone their art to such a level that this essential significance will come across to even the uninitiated viewer. The forms and styles that make up the tools of their trade should be a help rather than a hindrance in achieving this purpose. Thus if their technique is strong and true, the hearts of the men and women depicted in the plays of Bunraku will not fail to touch the heart of the viewer whether he be a novice or an expert.

The Shamisen Accompanist

Now let us take a look at the accompanying instrument. It is not unusual to hear a Shamisen Accompanist explaining after a performance that he left out or added notes or passages here and there to fit the specific mood or intensity of his Narrator. This is a clear indication of the solicitous attention and support constantly provided to the Bunraku Narrator by his Accompanist.

However, this does not mean that their adherance to tradition and precision of form is any less strict than that of the Narrators in terms of training and execution, for they must be equally familiar with the Narrators art and technique as with their own in order to provide such unfailing support in spite of any new tack the Narrator may take in a given performance.

The shamisen used in Bunraku is the largest of all the three instruments that go by that name in the classical performing arts. It is known as the *futo-zao* (literally 'thick neck'). The next smaller instrument is called the *chu-zao* and is used in Tokiwazu and Jiuta, while the smallest is called the *hoso-zao* and is used for Nagauta and Kouta.

The shamisen is played by holding the neck in the left hand and the plectrum in the right. The strings are pressed against the marks on the neck by the fingers of the left hand to control the pitch and the strings are stroked to make them resound by the plectrum in the right hand. In the process of intense training and practice, the forefinger of the left hand which comes into direct contact with the strings goes through a period of skin breakage and bleeding before hard callouses are finally formed. The same thing happens with the part of the right hand that comes into direct contact with the sharp edge of the plectrum and the point on the wrist of the left hand that rests against the body of the instrument. It is only when these callouses are firmly established that the shamisen musician attains the first level of mature artistry. And any extended neglect of sufficient regular rehearsal can very quickly result in a softening of these points and a sudden drop in technique. Also the nails of the fingers of the left hand that depress the strings must be very hard. Such care is taken by master musicians to maintain their hardness that they claim that they never let them come into direct contact with hot water even when they bathe.

But all these precautions are merely for the purpose of producing good sound quality. True artistry comes in the utilization of that sound to evoke specific time, mood, and character. For instance, though Princess Yaegaki in 'Twenty-Four Expressions of Filial Love' (*Honcho Nijushi Ko*), Hatsugiku in 'A Picture Book of the Taiko Tales' (*Ehon Taiko Ki*), and Osome in 'The New Ballad Singer' (*Shinpan Uta-zai-mon*) all fall into the general stock category of princesses or well-bred young ladies, the shamisen player must delineate their individual personalities by producing different sound textures for each in spite of the narrow range of sound types his instrument is capable of producing. Thus we see the important position he holds as an absolutely necessary support to the Narrator.

In terms of musical notation, the shamisen player is provided with very little guidance. The Narrator's libretto has a small red mark at the beginning of each passage which indicates one of the three types of narration — kotoba, jiai, or fushi — plus one of the three pitch marks which merely indicate low (*chu*), medium (*u*), or high (*haru*). But while the Narrator reads his libretto during performance the shamisen player is expected to have his music memorized, so he is deprived of even the minimal notation marks as an aid in actual performance.

Aside from the normal shamisen music, there are some plays in which the shamisen player uses a tea cup or a candlestick in place of his instrument to produce special sound effects, and others in which he flourishes his shamisen like a baton for comic effect.

The Puppeteers

Bunraku boasts the only three-man puppets in the world. French theatrician Jean-Louis Barrault is quoted often as having said that the Bunraku puppeteers are gods incarnate. And it is true indeed that when the team of three — the Chief Handler (*omo-zukai*), the Left Handler (*hidari-zukai*), and the Leg Handler (*ashi-zukai*) — achieve perfect timing and harmony of movement, the puppets appear to take on a life of their own that is truly mystical to behold.

A Bunraku puppet is made up of a head, a shoulder board, a trunk, arms, and legs. The Chief Handler takes the lead in manipulating a puppet. He wears tall boxlike clogs on his feet to raise him high enough to hold the puppet at the proper height above the stage railing to be seen by the audience. His clogs are fitted with thick straw soles to muffle the sound when he moves from place to place. He inserts his left hand into the opening in the puppet's lower back and grasps the small stick that supports the head to make it stand up straight on top of the shoulder board. Some of the larger puppets weigh as much as a human infant and this heavy mass must be supported entirely by the left arm of the Chief Handler. At the same time, he must use the five fingers of his left hand to pull the strings that control the nodding and the shaking of the head, the verticle and horizontal movements of the eyes, the raising and lowering of the eyebrows, and the opening and closing of the mouth to evoke the entire range of facial expressions. And on top of all this work for the left hand and arm, the Chief Handler must use his right hand to operate the right arm of the puppet as well. In order to keep the puppet sufficiently upright, the elbow of the left arm must be held quite high and at an extremely uncomfortable ninety degree angle. All in all, the work of the Chief Handler is quite exhausting physical labor.

The Left Handler manipulates the left arm of the puppet with his right hand. As a general rule, his left hand and arm are held straight against his own left side and hip, and he takes a position as close to the Chief Handler as possible at all times. However, in the case of a few particularly large male puppets, he uses his left arm to help the Chief Handler support the weight by placing his left hand under the puppet's left hip. The Left Handler is also responsible for caring for and making sure that all hand properties are in their proper places, and for carrying the

Chief Handler's boxlike clogs to and from the stage.

The Leg Handler stands in half crouching position with his hands grasping the rings on the heels of the puppet's feet in the case of male puppets, but for female puppets, which generally have no feet due to their long kimono skirts, he inserts his hands in the lower part of the skirts and moves them in such a way that the puppets appear to be using their feet and legs to walk, run, sit, kneel, or squat. The Leg Handler is also responsible for stamping his feet in time with the shamisen accompaniment for sound effects and accenting of rhythms and emotions. In spite of the fact that he is required to stand in a most uncomfortable position and that he is hardly ever seen by the audience, the Leg Handler must have a firm grasp of the music and the ability to sense the movements of the Chief Handler almost before they are made in order to do his job properly. Tradition says that it takes ten years of training to master the art of the Leg Handler, ten years more to become a skilled Left Handler, and another ten years to learn the techniques of the Chief Handler, with true mastery coming only after these 30 years of basic training have been completed.

As a general rule, all three puppeteers are dressed entirely in black, with black translucent hoods over their heads, but there are some plays in which the Chief Handler raises his hood to reveal his face to the audience, and upon very special celebratory occasions, they don very colorful formal costumes and leave heads and faces completely bare. There are also a very small number of super-special pieces for which all three puppeteers bare their faces. One of the most famous of these is the flamboyant role of Benkei in 'The Subscription List' (*Kanjincho*).

In any case, it is the well-timed teamwork of the three puppeteers that seems to instill independent life into the puppets and fascinate the viewer with an illusion of detailed and poignant reality.

The Puppet Heads

The heads of Bunraku and the masks of Noh are two elements of the traditional theater arts of Japan that draw a great deal of interest outside of the context of the arts in which they are used. But here their similarity ends, for they stand in sharp contrast with each other in terms of both intent and means of expression. The Noh mask exists somewhere between life and death in a world of deep and subtle expression. Emotions seem to flit across their surfaces with the slightest change of angle. Raising the face suggests joy and lowering it evokes a sense of sadness, and so forth. But the Bunraku head is clearly alive and explicit. Its eyes move in all directions, its eyebrows can be raised and lowered, its mouth opens and closes, and there are even some comic heads in which the nose is capable of moving.

The Noh mask is highly revered as one of Japan's greatest art genres. When not in use on the stage, they are wrapped carefully in silk and put away in special wooden boxes. But the Bunraku head has never been honored in any way, and they can be seen hanging in nonchalant rows on the walls of the puppeteers' dressing rooms when not in use.

Thus we see, through these tools of the two arts, the contrasting nature of the art forms as a whole. Noh is profound and aristocratic, while Bunraku is broad, brash, and overt, remaining very much an entertainment for the masses.

The heads used for period pieces are normally larger and more imposing than those used for domestic dramas. The head immediately reveals the personality traits of a character, with whiteness and smallness standing for goodness and reds, purples, and grays standing for basic evil.

Altogether there are about 70 different types of heads, among which male heads are in the great majority. The bulk of them are character types that can be used for a number of roles, but there are some that are designated for a single famous character. For example, there is the special head for the aged blind Heike warrior Kagekiyo (Photo 95), and the female demon called Gabu (Photo 108) that can change from a beautiful woman to a terrifying apparition of evil with huge fangs, glaring gold eyes, and sharp horns in an instant. Those that can be used for a number of roles change in appearance through the application of wigs, makeup and costumes of specific roles. Some roles change heads during the process of a play depending on the state of mind of the character in a given scene. For instance, the brave warrior priest Benkei is normally given the O-danshichi head, but in the famous piece called 'The Subscription List' (*Kanjincho* — Photo 66), he is given the Bunshichi head (Photo 104) to stress his rational intelligence that is revealed in that particular situation.

The following photos show the character types of some of the heads.

106 — Ugly Young Woman *(Ofuku)*   107 — Old Woman *(Baba)*

108 — Evil Old Woman *(Aku-baba)*   109 — Femal Demon *(Gabu)*

102 — Priest *(Shonin)*

103 — The Stutterer *(Matahei)*

104 — Stern Older Man *(Kiichi)*

105 — Mature Man *(Bunshichi)*

The Stage

The special structure of the Bunraku stage (Photo 109) was designed to facilitate the movement of the puppets and their handlers.

The low black wall near the audience is called the 'First Railing.' The 'Second Railing' stands beyond the first at a height of 85cm. It is behind this Second Railing that most of the action takes place. The 'Third Railing' divides the performance area into two sections. When a scene takes place both indoors and out, the indoor section is behind the Third Railing and the outdoor part is between the Second and Third Railings.

The backdrop scenery is sometimes fitted with special rollers so that in a travel scene, the characters walk or run in place while the scene behind them unrolls to show their progress through the countryside.

A small revolving platform known as the toko is attached to the down stage left edge of the main stage. It is here that the Narrator and his Shamisen Accompanist perform. There is an upper level on this platform which is covered by a hanging bamboo blind. This second storey is used by less skilled narrators and shamisen players when they perform, to keep them hidden from the view of the audience.

As a general rule (as is true in all Japanese classiscal theater) entrances and exists are made from stage left. Part of the reason for this practice in Bunraku is due to the fact that it does not look good for the Left Handler to be in front of the Chief Handler, particularly for entrances.

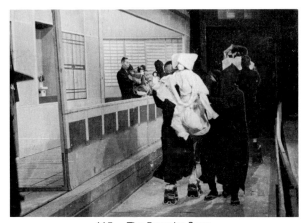

115 — The Bunraku Stage

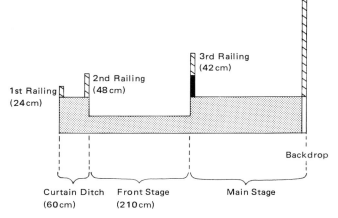

1st Railing
(24 cm)

2nd Railing
(48 cm)

3rd Railing
(42 cm)

Backdrop

Curtain Ditch
(60 cm)

Front Stage
(210 cm)

Main Stage

THE HISTORY OF BUNRAKU

The art of Bunraku puppet theatre developed as an entertainment medium of the common people.

Japan's mainstream traditional arts are Noh, Kyogen, Joruri (or Bunraku), and Kabuki. Noh and Kyogen are medieval theatre forms. Noh is a masked drama of song and dance. It presents romantic tales of old Japan against the background of Buddhism in a highly symbolic and stylized form. In direct contrast, Kyogen is a theatre of healthy humor drawn from the daily plebian lifestyle of the Muromachi Period (1394-1466).

Joruri began as a narrative art that falls somewhere between singing and dramatic storytelling accompanied by the banjolike shamisen. It was much later that puppets were added to form what we know today as Bunraku. The early Joruri was heavily influenced by the chanting of the Noh Drama, but its subject matter and manner of presentation were closer to the lives of the people and more realistic. Different from the other early modern theatre style called Kabuki in which the performer takes precedence over the script, the Joruri narrator is never allowed to deviate from his text in even the slightest detail. Equally strict adherence to form is also required of the Bunraku puppeteers. In fact, the traditions are considered of such absolute importance in Bunraku and Joruri that there was a time when performers were forbidden to attend performances of Kabuki for fear of a detrimental influence on their own art, since there is a great deal of overlap in use of scripts by the two arts.

The narrative tradition in Japan is extremely old. All classical literature including THE TALES OF ISE, THE

TALES OF THE HEIKE, and THE RISE AND FALL OF THE GENJI AND HEIKE CLANS was born of the wandering blind minstrels who accompanied themselves on the lutelike biwa. Such minstrels began to flourish during the 10th and 11th centuries.

The most popular piece of minstrelsy during medieval times was THE TALE OF PRINCESS JORURI. It is a highly idealized and complicated story of love between the 14 year old scion of the Genji Clan named Ushiwaka (later to become the famed general Yoshitsune) and the 13 year old daughter of a wealthy family of Yahagi in Mikawa whose name was Princess Joruri. It was presented in 12 long sections for which reason it was also known as THE TWELVE SCENE JORURI STORYBOOK.

By the end of the 15th century the overwhelming popularity of this tale resulted in the entire art of narrative storytelling coming to be known as 'Joruri.' About that same time, a famed Joruri narrator named Ishimura brought a banjolike instrument from the Ryukyu Islands that was covered with snake skin and played by plucking the strings with the fingernails. It was called the Jamisen. He remodelled it with a cover of cat skin and a plectrum for stroking the strings and renamed it the Shamisen.

The use of the new Shamisen in place of the old Biwa gave added life to the art and its popularity spread throughout the entire nation. By the middle of the 16th century, the Joruri Narrators and their Shamisen Accompanists were joined by puppeteers known as Kugutsushi, bringing into being the conglomerate art we know today as Joruri Puppet Theatre or Bunraku.

The first two narrators to make the new conglomerate art successful in both eastern and western Japan were

Sugimoto Tango-no-jo and Satsuma Joun (later to change his name to Satsuma-dayu). They both traveled from Kyoto to Edo where they established the first Edo style Joruri. Their students were responsible for creating the numerous styles that remain a part of Japanese dramatic narrative music today, Bizen Bushi and Koto Bushi were created by students of Tango-no-jo and the broad and outlandish Kinpira Bushi was the work of Joun's student Izumi-dayu (later to take the name Sakurai Tango-no-jo). It was from the family of Izumi-dayu that the originator of the broad 'aragoto' style of Edo Kabuki Ichikawa Danjuro was born, and the Kinpira Bushi influence is in strong evidence in his style of acting. Other styles that were born of the same lines include Bunya, Itchu, Tokiwazu, Shinnai, and Kiyomoto.

Finally a student of Joun named Toraya Gen-dayu went back to the Kansai area and established himself in Kyoto, after which one of his students named Inoue Harima-no-jo moved to Osaka where his lively, strong style made him extremely popular with the citizens of that great commercial center. During the same period one of his second generation students named Uji Kaga-no-jo settled in Kyoto where he created a softer, more lyrical style which appealed to the more aristocratic tastes of the citizens of that old capital city. Thus began an intense rivalry between the Joruri puppet theatres of the two cities.

The people of Kyoto were strongly attracted to the Noh Drama, more because of its position as the exclusive property of the ruling military elite than from actual knowledge or interest in it. It seems that the entire art of Joruri was heavily influenced by the Noh Drama, but Kaga-no-jo was particularly clear in his dependence upon the Noh Drama as his source, typified by his statement 'Joruri has no ultimate teacher, but we must keep in mind the fact that Noh chanting (*utai*) is the parent of our art.' Thus true to his chosen home, his aim was toward a highly intellectual, refined Joruri style.

The Osaka scene was, on the other hand, quite different. Harima-no-jo's student Shimizu Rihei discovered a young farmer from Osaka's Tennoji area whose voice had a natural resonance and fullness. Rehei took this farm boy named Gorobei on as a student and gave him the professional name of Ri-dayu. His natural talents allowed him to learn with amazing speed. Before long he had mastered the strong Harima Bushi style and had moved to Kyoto to study the elegant style of Kaga-no-jo, after which he went on to study the 'tear-jerking' Bunya Bushi style. After gaining confidence in all the styles popular at the time, Ridayu changed his name to Takemoto Gidayu and took Osaka by storm with the new individualistic style he had created as a result of his broad range of training. Osaka was a town where originality and skill were valued above background and connections. Gidayu was a true son of this his hometown, and his attitude of insisting that his own original style, based upon training in all the old forms, was the only true Joruri, made him dear to the hearts of his fellow townsmen.

Gidayu's attitude was in diametric opposition to that of Kaga-no-jo and his elite Kyoto following. While Kaga-no-jo's position was strong, Gidayu took over and completely dominated the art after the opening of his own theatre called the Takemoto-za in the Dotonbori area of Osaka in 1684. His domination was so complete that subsequent generations ignored the old styles even to the extent of calling the art Gidayu instead of Joruri from that time forward.

Gidayu's domination of the art of Bunraku can be at least partially attributed to his use of the fine scripts of playwright Chikamatsu Monzaemon who is often referred to as the 'Shakespeare of Japan.'

Chikamatsu died at the age of 72 on November 22, 1724. Very little is known for certain about where he was born or where he was buried. Of course, there are many legends that have grown up around him, many of which conflict with each other, and several different temples have graves with his name on them.

113 — Portrait of
Chikamatsu Monzaemon

114 — Portrait of
Takemoto Gidayu

The most widely accepted theory is that his real name was Sugimori Nobumori, that his father was originally a member of the Echizen Clan, and that in his younger days, Chikamatsu served as a retainer of the aristocratic Ichijo family. His early training and interest in writing plays is said to have come from his connection with that noble family, the head of which was a fairly well known Joruri playwright himself.

Chikamatsu first appears in clearly recorded history as a playwright for Kaga-no-Jo, but he soon took a strong interest in Gidayu's work and began writing for him instead. His first play for Gidayu was 'Kagekiyo's Success' (*Shusse Kagekiyo*). There was a short period of time later on in his life when he wrote exclusively for the Kyoto Kabuki actor Sakata Tojuro, but he soon lost patience with the revisions made by live actors to suit their own whims and returned to the puppet theatre for which he continued to write for the remainder of his life. During his lifetime, Chikamatsu wrote 90 some period pieces and 24 contemporary dramas.

Chikamatsu expressed the true human situation with all its strengths and weaknesses as found in the midst of the contradictions of feudal society, and this he did with living words and a unique love for humanity. Live actors constantly strive to bring their own expressive abilities into a role which often draws them far afield from the intent of the playwright. On the other hand, puppets are capable of expressing all the human emotions while remaining devoid of any detracting egoism. It was for this reason that Chikamatsu chose Bunraku over Kabuki for the presentation of his masterpieces.

Thus Gidayu was blessed with the exclusive rights on

the new works of Japan's greatest playwright, but strangely enough, this improvement only served to put him deep into debt by 1703. In an attempt to regain popularity with the public, Chikamatsu broke into the fresh territory of the contemporary drama with his 'Double Suicide at Sonezaki' (*Sonezaki Shinju* – Photos 49-52). Everyday life of the common man had been presented before in Japan in Kyogen, but it was camouflaged in humor. Thus, Chikamatsu was the first Japanese playwright to take a serious look at the tragedy of life under the severe restrictions of contemporary society. His new play attracted the attention of the people with its relevance to their own lives. It was such a commercial success that the Takemoto-za was completely out of debt almost immediately and Chikamatsu was firmly established from that point to the present as Japan's greatest playwright of all times.

The main result of this creative activity was the establishment of two dramatic genres which were firmly based upon the viewpoint of the townsmen of the day. They were the historical romances within which a glimpse of real life problems were presented, and the contemporary dramas of life in feudal Japan with its ever present confrontation between duty and emotion.

Beginning in 1706, Gidayu placed the management of his theatre in the hands of Takeda Izumo who proved to be a truly brilliant manager-producer. Gidayu himself concentrated on performance from that time forward. Also Chikamatsu moved from Kyoto to Osaka for the purpose of serving more effectively as full time playwright for Gidayu's theatre. This team of greats went on to make numerous improvements in all aspects of their art, resulting in great success for their Takemoto-za in the ensuing years.

Just prior to the presentation of 'Double Suicide at Sonezaki' (*Sonezaki Shinju*), a popular young narrator named Takemoto Uneme had broken away from the Takemoto-za and taken the name Toyotake Waka-dayu. His new Toyotake-za proved a serious rival to the older theatre. The rich but subtle style of the Takemoto-za came to be known as the 'Western Style' while the broader, brighter, more melodic style of the Toyotake-za was called the 'Eastern Style.' While competition between the two theatres was high, still both drew large crowds due to their care in chosing pieces that fit their own style, so that avid fans tended to patronize both groups enthusiastically.

Gidayu I died in 1714, and he was succeeded by the 24 year old Masa-dayu, whose style was brought to full effect in Chikamatsu's brilliant new period drama 'The Battle of Kokusenya' (*Kokusenya Kassen* – Photo 58) which was premiered in 1715 and went on to set a new long-run record of 17 months. Chikamatsu was further inspired by Masa-dayu to write such great masterpieces as 'Double Suicide at Ten-no-Amijima' (*Shinju Ten-no-Amijima* – Photos 54-57) and 'Murder of a Woman in a Hell of Oil' (*Onna-Goroshi Abura no Jigoku* – Photo 93) during his later years.

Later on a puppeteer named Tatsumatsu Hachirobei left the Toyotake-za to form his own troupe with Ki-no-Kaion as playwright. After a number of years of struggling, success was realized with the premier in 1726 and subsequent 2 year run of Kaion's 'Chronicle of Hojo Tokiyori' (*Hojo Jirai Ki*).

Ki-no-Kaion remains in history as a minor playwright due to his didactic style resulting from his scholarly background in history and poetry. However, during their lifetimes, he and Chikamatsu vied for popularity and his works provided effective competition with those of the master playwright.

After the death of Chikamatsu and Kaion, great changes were seen in the art of Bunraku. It was in 1734 that puppeteer Yoshida Bunzaburo devised the three-man puppeteering system that is the mainstay of the art today. He shocked the public with the versatility of this new puppeteering style in the Shinoda Wood Scene of Act 2 of 'The Ouchi Tale of Ashiya Doman' (*Ashiya Doman Ouchi Kagami* — Photos 80-81). The three-man puppeteering style was presented in this scene in the handling of two rowdy messengers (*yakko*). Enthusiastic audience reaction brought about subsequent improvements in detailed movement for eyes, mouths, eyebrows, and fingers until this art of puppetry reached its zenith with the presentation of the naked Danshichi in 'The Tale of the Summer Festival in Osaka' (*Natsu Matsuri Naniwa Kagami* — Photo 67) in 1745. It was during this same period that the demand for more spectacle and greater versatility gave birth to the practice of having a number of playwrights cooperate in the writing of a single play. Major playwrights from this period include Takeda Izumo, Bunkodo, and Miyoshi Shoraku. The masterpieces they left to posterity include 'Moralistic Tales of Sugawara Michizane' (*Sugawara Denju Tenarai Kagami* — Photos 61-62), 'Proper Upbringing of a Young Lady at Mount Imose' (*Imose Yama Onna Teikin* — Photos 20-26), 'Twenty-Four Expressions of Filial Love' (*Honcho Niju-*

shi Ko — Photos 41-44), and 'The Faithful Forty-Seven' (*Kana-dehon Chushingura* — Photo 2-19).

Finally the Takemoto-za closed its doors to bring an end to its brilliant 84 year long history in 1767. It had been preceeded by the closing of the 63 year history of the Toyotake-za two years earlier in 1765. Thus ended the great period of development and success of the puppet theatre art which we know today as Bunraku.

However, there remains one more historical incident of import to the early days of the art. That was the appearance of a man from Awaji Island named Uemura Bunraku-ken. He had come to Osaka some time earlier, but his first public appearance on the puppet drama scene came with his opening of a theatre in 1805. He began a line of brilliant puppet theatre producers and it was Bunraku-ken III who first opened a theatre with the name of Bunraku-za. This took place in 1872, and it has been since that date that the art has been known as "Bunraku.'

The modern history of Bunraku has been a series of violent ups and downs. During the final two decades of the 18th century and the first decade of the 19th century, a number of theatres were built and burned down, and several splinter groups formed and disappeared among the performers.

It was in 1909 that the Shochiku Entertainment Company purchased performance rights and set out to gather all Bunraku artists under its umbrella, resulting in a reasonable level of prosperity for the art until its theatres and many of its puppets were destroyed in the

1945 Osaka air raids.

Shochiku made concerted efforts to effect a revival of Bunraku as soon as the war ended, culminating in the opening of a newly built Bunraku-za in February 1946.

Then on June 14, 1947, Bunraku enjoyed the greatest honor in its entire history in the form of a command performance for Emperor Hirohito. Every effort was made to show the art at its best for the occasion. The program consisted of the Shigenoi Parts with Her Child Scene from Act 10 of 'A Colorful Bridle for a Beloved Wife' (*Koi Nyobo Somewake Tazuna* — Photo 77) and the Mount Yoshino Travel Scene from Act 4 of 'Yoshitsune and the Thousand Cherry Trees' (*Yoshitune Senbon-Zakura* — Photos 27-33 and Cover Photo).

It was also during 1947 that the younger performers formed a union to demand better pay and working conditions, splitting the art into two factions with the older traditionalists insisting that artists must not carry on like laborers.

After the death of the Shochiku producer Shirai Shojiro, who had been the staunchest supporter and promoter of Bunraku's traditions, efforts by the company to make a financial success of Bunraku took new directions. The old theatre was abandoned due to its inconvenient location and a new one was built in the busy Doton-bori area in 1956.

The two factions within the art were reunited under the roof of this new Doton-bori Bunraku-za, and a number of ambitious original pieces were presented. These included adaptations of such Western dramatic material as 'Hamlet,' 'Madame Butterfly,' and 'Camille,' along with borrowings from Shinpa and dramatizations of contemporary Japanese literature and films. But the only lasting effect of these efforts during the late 1950s was the re-introduction into the permanent repertoire of a few classical pieces that had been ignored for some time, such as "Double Suicide at Sonezaki' (*Sonezaki Shinju* — Photos 49-52) and "Murder of a Woman in a Hell of Oil' (*Onna-Goroshi Abura no Jigoku* — Photo 93).

Continued financial difficulties and internal disharmony between the two factions finally led Shochiku to throw up its hands in despair and give up all production rights. Thus Bunraku was faced with total disappearance. But such official organizations as the National Government, Osaka Prefecture, NHK, and Kansai Area financial circles provided funds for the reorganization of the art as the incorporated body called the Bunraku Association. Under this banner, the two artistic factions resolved all their mutual disagreements and the name of their theatre was changed to the Asahi-za.

Then Japan's National Theatre was built in 1966, providing a Tokyo home for the art of Bunraku in its Small Hall. And it has enjoyed a steadily growing popularity both at home and abroad since that time.

INDEX OF PLAY TITLES

HOIKUSHA COLOR BOOKS

ENGLISH EDITIONS

Book Size 4″×6″

COLORED ILLUSTRATIONS FOR NATURALISTS

Text in Japanese, with index in Latin or English.

First Issues (Book Size 6″ × 8″)

1. BUTTERFLIES of JAPAN
2. INSECTS of JAPAN vol.1
3. INSECTS of JAPAN vol.2
4. SHELLS of JAPAN vol.1
5. FISHES of JAPAN vol.1
6. BIRDS of JAPAN
7. MAMMALS of JAPAN
8. SEA SHORE ANIMALS of JAPAN
9. GARDEN FLOWERS vol.1
10. GARDEN FLOWERS vol.2
11. ROSES and ORCHIDS
12. ALPINE FLORA of JAPAN vol.1
13. ROCKS
14. ECONOMIC MINERALS
15. HERBACEOUS PLANTS of JAPAN vol.1
16. HERBACEOUS PLANTS of JAPAN vol.2
17. HERBACEOUS PLANTS of JAPAN vol.3
18. SEAWEEDS of JAPAN
19. TREES and SHRUBS of JAPAN
20. EXOTIC AQUARIUM FISHES vol.1
21. MOTHS of JAPAN vol.1
22. MOTHS of JAPAN vol.2
23. FUNGI of JAPAN vol.1
24. PTERIDOPHYTA of JAPAN
25. SHELLS of JAPAN vol.2
26. FISHES of JAPAN vol.2
27. EXOTIC AQUARIUM FISHES vol.2
28. ALPINE FLORA of JAPAN vol.2
29. FRUITS
30. REPTILES and AMPHIBIANS of JAPAN
31. ECONOMIC MINERALS vol.2
32. FRESHWATER FISHES of JAPAN
33. GARDEN PLANTS of the WORLD vol.1
34. GARDEN PLANTS of the WORLD vol.2
35. GARDEN PLANTS of the WORLD vol.3
36. GARDEN PLANTS of the WORLD vol.4
37. GARDEN PLANTS of the WORLD vol.5
38. THE FRESHWATER PLANKTON of JAPAN
39. MEDICINAL PLANTS of JAPAN

<**ENGLISH EDITIONS**>

SHELLS
OF
THE
WESTERN
PACIFIC
IN
COLOR

Book Size 7″×10″

⟨vol. I⟩ by Tetsuaki Kira
(304 pages, 72 in color)
⟨vol. II⟩ by Tadashige Habe
(304 pages, 66 in color)

FISHES
OF
JAPAN
IN
COLOR

Book Size 7″×10″

by Toshiji Kamohara
(210 pages, 64 in color)